100 THINGS
YOU NEED TO KNOW
IF YOU OWN A QUILT:

A QUILT OWNER'S MANUAL

Located in Paducah, Kentucky, the American Quilter's Society (AQS) is dedicated to promoting the accomplishments of today's quilters. Through its publications and events, AQS strives to honor today's quiltmakers and their work and to inspire future creativity and innovation in quiltmaking.

EDITOR: LINDA BAXTER LASCO
GRAPHIC DESIGN: AMY CHASE
COVER DESIGN: MICHAEL BUCKINGHAM
PHOTOGRAPHY: CHARLES R. LYNCH

Library of Congress Cataloging-in-Publication Data
Hazelwood, Ann.
  100 things you need to know if you own a quilt: a quilt owner's manual / by Ann Hazelwood.
    p. cm.
Summary: "This guide to quilt ownership includes tips on provenance, buying and selling, displaying, cleaning, storing, and caring for quilts. Illustrated with prizewinning quilts from the 2006 and 2007 American Quilter's Society Show and Contest." Provided by publisher.
  ISBN 978-1-57432-946-9
1. Quilts—Collectors and collecting—Handbooks, manuals, etc. 2. Quilts—Cleaning—Handbooks, manuals, etc. 3. Quilts—Conservation and restoration—Handbooks, manuals, etc. I. American Quilter's Society. II. Title. III Title: One hundred things to know if you own a quilt. IV. Title: Hundred things to know if you own a quilt.

NK9112.H39 2007
746.46.028'8—dc22

2007022828

Additional copies of this book may be ordered from the American Quilter's Society, PO Box 3290, Paducah, KY 42002-3290; 800-626-5420 (orders only please); or online at www.AmericanQuilter.com. For all other inquiries, please call 270-898-7903.

Dedication

Each and every day of my life I have lived with quilts. Growing up with quilts to snuggle in, then learning to make them, gave me a career in the quilting industry.

I dedicate this book to my mother, Esther Marie Meyer, who died when I was sixteen years of age. She was an avid quiltmaker who first exposed me to the feel and beauty of quilts. I regret that she did not live to see my love for quilts evolve. She would appreciate my passing on my knowledge and love of quilts to others so that they too can enjoy living with quilts.

PEARLS FROM GRANDMA, 88" x 88", Tammy Finkler, Conklin, MI

Contents

ROSES FOR MATTIE, 82" x 82", Irma Gail Hatcher, Conway, AR

GETTING TO KNOW YOU

PROVENANCE

Knowing who made your quilt and where it came from may add to its value. Provenance is information on the origin and history of an item. Provenance on a quilt is a combination birth certificate and résumé. When was the quilt made (the birth), who made it (the parent), what is it made of (the ethnicity), and where has it been since (the life story)?

Every piece of information about your quilt is important for future generations. Get to know your quilt like you would get to know a new friend.

UP CLOSE AND PERSONAL

Take a good close look at your quilt and at its condition. Examine both the front and the back.

Embroidered or quilted names, dates, or initials, often found around the edges of the quilt, can give you tantalizing details about your quilt's history.

LOOK, LOOK, I SEE It!, 46" x 41½", Anna Faustino, North Arlington, NJ

AUTUMN FLOWER PARK, 83" x 95", Kimi Aoki, Chikuma, Nagano, Japan

DOCUMENTATION

Collect all the information you can about your quilt—who made it, how they made it, when, where, out of what materials, and for what purpose. Knowing where it's been and who has owned it is also part of its history. Include a photo of the entire quilt and at least one close-up shot.

Other items of interest would be an appraisal, sales receipt, pattern, templates, fabric samples, information about the quiltmaker, where the quilt has been exhibited, and any recognition it may have received (such as awards, inclusion in books or magazines, or appearances on TV).

SMILE FOR THE CAMERA

One of the most important ways to document your quilt is by photographing it. A photograph will prove its existence and its condition, should theft or damage occur.

Be sure to get close-up shots of any special features such as the signature of a famous person, an embroidered name or date, or some particularly fine quilting. Save the photographs with the rest of your quilt documentation.

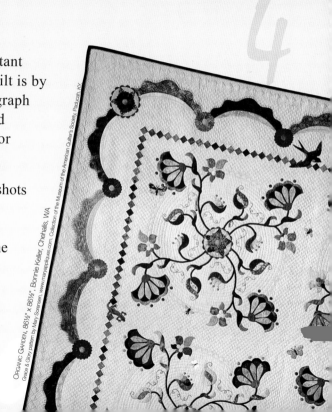

ORGANIC GARDEN, 86½" x 86½", Bonnie Keller, Chehalis, WA
Grace & Glory pattern by Mary Sorenson, www.marysapplques.com. Collection of the Museum of the American Quilter's Society, Paducah, KY

FLORAL FANTASY, 90" x 112", West Pasco Quilters Guild, Inc., Hudson, FL
Patterns by Dianne Johnston, Cooloolabin, Queensland, Australia
www.diannejohnstonproducts.com.au

WHAT'S IN A NAME?

Your quilt can have more than one name.

What is the name of the pattern? There are thousands of traditional pattern names and sometimes different names for the same pattern.

What is the title of the quilt? The quiltmaker may have named the quilt, just like an artist names a painting or an author titles a book.

Either of these names more closely describe your quilt.

WHAT'S YOUR TYPE?

A quilt can be described by its type, which indicates the overall technique used to make it.

An appliquéd quilt is one where pieces of fabric are sewn onto a larger background fabric. The pieces are typically rounded and softer-edged than in a pieced quilt. The technique lends itself to florals and pictorial subjects.

A pieced quilt features lots of fabric bits sewn together edge-to-edge. In their simplest form, they are made of easily recognizable geometric shapes that fit together like the pieces of a puzzle.

A quilt that combines both appliqué and piecing is described as having mixed techniques.

A wholecloth quilt, as the name suggests, is made of one fabric where the design is in the quilting and not from piecing or appliqué.

STYLE

A quilt's style refers to its overall design or layout, not the name of its pattern or the technique used to make it. There is a wide variety of styles with new ones being created all the time by today's creative quiltmakers.

Some standard examples include the *sampler* quilt, which generally consists of many different blocks, each made with a different pattern or quilting design. A *medallion* quilt will have a large central design with a series of borders surrounding it. A *charm* quilt is made with pieces all of the same size and shape, each one of a different fabric. A *crazy* quilt incorporates many different sizes and shapes of pieces, usually of non-traditional quilt fabrics (such as silks, satins, and velvets) that are heavily embroidered and embellished.

LIFE IN HOLLY RIDGE, 76" x 53", Nancy Prince, Orlando, FL

STYLE BY MAKER

Some quiltmakers are so prolific with such distinctive styles that quilts by others that seem to mimic their style will be described as being in that particular quiltmaker's style. The quiltmaker's name identifies the style.

PATTERN NAME

There are references listing common patterns and their names. You can use them to identify your quilt's pattern name.

Nebraska's Rising Sun, 84½" x 85", Sandi McMillan & Laura Franchini, Albion, NE

AND WHAT DO YOU DO?

A quilt can be described by its purpose. A utilitarian quilt is made to be used. It will probably spend time on a bed or wrapped around a child or chilly television watcher.

A quilt acquired as part of a collection will be treated quite differently from a utilitarian quilt. It will be displayed or exhibited, rather than used, and might possibly be stored away for most of the time to protect it.

Other quilts may be made or purchased simply because they add just the right touch to your décor.

Quilts for Causes

Some organizations sponsor the making of quilts for fundraising and to raise awareness of or honor the victims of a particular disease. AIDS, breast cancer, and Alzheimer's disease are among the most well-known of these causes.

Fundraising

Quilts are often used for fundraising by quilt, church, and civic groups. The members will make a quilt and sell raffle tickets for a chance to win the quilt.

SIGNATURE QUILTS

In the past, money was sometimes raised making a quilt with plain sections in each block where people could pay to sign their names. Signatures of friends and family make quilts personal.

SWISH & SWIRL, 46" x 46", Susan Nelson, Prior Lake, MN

MEMORIAL QUILTS

Quilts made to
memorialize people who
have passed away are
often constructed from
the clothing of the loved
one. Today's technology
enables us to transfer
photographs to fabric and
these, too, can become
part of a memorial quilt.

BLESSING, 85" x 85", Ikuko Hagino, Yokohama, Kanagawa, Japan

FUNERAL QUILTS

Some quilts are designed specifically to cover caskets at funerals. Even casket linings with quilt patterns are commercially available.

HOW'D THEY DO THAT?

How a quilt was made is an important detail. Quilts made entirely by hand have always been highly regarded. Quilts pieced or appliquéd by machine can be just as appealing and exquisitely done.

Tight, close stitches in the seam lines usually indicate machine piecing. A V-like look to the stitches in the seam lines indicates hand piecing.

HAND VERSUS MACHINE QUILTING

Hand quilting has generally been thought of as having greater value than machine quilting. However, machine quilting by an accomplished machine quilter can be just as highly regarded as quilting done by hand.

The *quality* of the quilting may well be more important than the method by which it was accomplished.

BUCKSKIN, 78" x 79", Marla Yeager, Ava, MO. Collection of the Museum of the American Quilter's Society, Paducah, KY.

SIZE MATTERS

A quilt can be described by its size. The size of a quilt is often an indication of its purpose and the naming is intuitive.

Large quilts made for beds are called (Surprise!) bed quilts.

Crib quilts, baby quilts, and doll quilts . . . self-explanatory.

A wall quilt is destined to hang on a wall, as are art quilts, even though some are big enough to cover a bed.

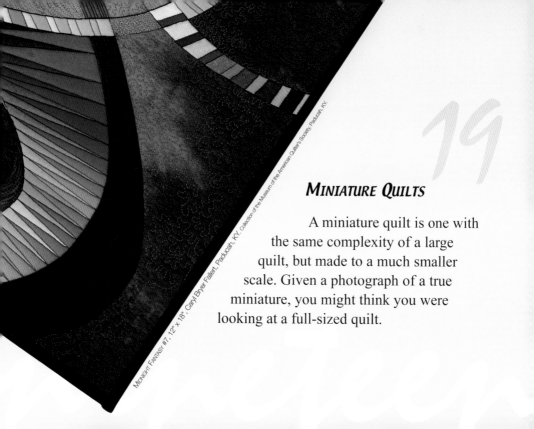

MINIATURE QUILTS

A miniature quilt is one with the same complexity of a large quilt, but made to a much smaller scale. Given a photograph of a true miniature, you might think you were looking at a full-sized quilt.

MIDNIGHT FANTASY #7, 12" x 18", Caryl Bryer Fallert, Paducah, KY. Collection of the Museum of the American Quilter's Society, Paducah, KY.

So Big!

Standard quilt sizes tend to be dictated by the commercial sizing of quilt batts. Although they can vary by a few inches among manufacturers, these are the available sizes.

Craft	34" x 45"
Crib or Baby	45" x 60"
Twin	72" x 92"
Full or Double	96" x 96"
Queen	92" x 108"
Super Queen	92" x 120"
King	121" x 121"

Too Much of a Good Thing

Beware a new, super-thick mattress! It may be called one size but may need a quilt the next size larger to cover it completely.

Hello, My Name Is . . .

Just as you'd put a name tag on a child, you want to put a label on your quilt so if it wanders off, people will be able to identify it and get it back to you.

Make a label of cloth and use a permanent, acid-free marker to write the name of the quilt, the maker, and your name and address. Sew the label onto the back side of your quilt.

Labels can be as elaborate as one cares to make them. You can embroider the information on cloth or print the information directly onto fabric that is stabilized and cut to fit through an ink-jet printer.

WATERMELON WINE, 55" x 69", Ruth Powers, Carbondale, KS

HOW OLD ARE YOU NOW?

When it comes to the value of a quilt, age is a factor, and a good one at that. The older a quilt is, the more valuable it may prove to be. The mitigating factor is its condition. Fabrics in their original state are valued more highly than those that are worn or faded.

Textiles over the age of 100 are considered "antique." The tem "vintage" can be used to describe fabrics that are not old enough to be called "antique."

DINNER AND A MOVIE?

Dating a quilt can be done in a number of ways. Unless you have precise and reliable information about its origin, you need to do some detective work to figure out how old your quilt is.

You may not be able to pinpoint exactly when a quilt was made, but a collection of clues will help you determine the probable age of a quilt.

A TRIUMPH OF TULIPS, 52" x 43", Melody Johnson, Cary, IL. Collection of Joan Franz.

AGE BY STYLE

A quilt's style can be a clue to its age. Baltimore Album quilts flourished in the 1840s. Quilts made from feed sacks were common during the Depression era. Crazy quilts were popular during Victorian times.

AGE BY HISTORICAL EVENT

A quilt's subject matter could be a clue to when it was made. If a quilt commemorates a particular historical event, you know it can't precede that date in time. Many quilts were made to acknowledge the United States centennial during the 1870s. The same was true during the country's bicentennial. The 1970s also marks the resurgence of quiltmaking's popularity that continues unabated today.

LOG CABIN/KALEIDOSCOPE, 84" x 84", Fumiko Ohkawa, Kobe, Hyogo, Japan

AGE BY MATERIALS

The type of batting can be an indication of age. Hold an old quilt up to the light and you may be able to see flecks in the batting.

A quilt can not be older than the newest material it contains. A quilt with poly-blend fabrics can't have been made before the 1940s.

PART OF A TREND

What's in, what's out, what's popular, and what's not can all affect what kinds of quilts are being made at any given time.

When the color known as turkey red was made dyefast in the 1880s, red and white quilts became extremely popular. Patriotic quilts are also common during times of war.

Your quilt may well be part of a trend, which can further identify its time and place.

TRIBUTE TO FELIX, 71½" x 89", Fleda Collins, Talbott, TN. Border from Appliqué Masterpiece: *Little Brown Bird* by Margaret Docherty, American Quilter's Society; appliqué pattern by Jeana Kimball, Foxglove Cottage Design Series, Spring City, UT.

Historically Big

Quilts often reflect the size of the beds of their time. In the mid-1800s, beds were very high, often requiring bed steps to climb up onto them. Very large quilts were made to accommodate that size. "Hired hand" quilts were long and narrow, made to cover the bunk beds hired hands slept on.

A three-quarter size bed was marketed during the Depression era, leading to an odd-sized bed quilt that was less than useful in later times. The twentieth century brought the advent of queen- and then king-size beds and quilts sized to cover them.

Your quilt's size may well be an indication of when it was made.

WILDFIRE! 41" x 54", Brenda Smith, Flagstaff, AZ

BRING IN THE PROFESSIONALS

There are appraisers educated and tested specifically on appraising quilts. There are three different reasons for a quilt appraisal. An *insurance appraisal* determines how much it would cost to replace a quilt, should it be lost or stolen. A *fair market appraisal* is an approximation of the price a knowledgeable buyer and seller would agree to for a given quilt. If a quilt is to be given as a donation, a *donation appraisal* can be done to establish the value for tax purposes.

Your own work on provenance and documentation will help an appraiser, who will be able to give you details on the materials, the pattern, and the time at which the quilt was made.

WHEN AUTUMN LEAVES START TO FALL, 80" x 93", Brenda Tower Jennings, Columbus, OH

LIVING QUARTERS

IT'S ALIVE!

"Plastics" may have been the best advice for *The Graduate*, but they're not the best thing for your quilt. A quilt is a living, breathing entity. Don't smother it by storing it in an air-tight container or a plastic bag. The old tradition of "airing the quilts" had a purpose that is still valid today. Your quilt will thrive on an occasional dose of fresh air.

It's tempting to want to use Velcro® products to hang a quilt, but these, too, are plastic and can damage your quilt over time.

HUMMINGBIRDS HEAVEN, 88½" x 110", Mary E. Piper, Racine, WI
Hummingbirds & Flowers pattern by Patricia Cox of One-of-a-Kind Quilting Designs

32

HUMIDITY

Your quilt may appear to be
perfectly dry, but even a tiny bit
of moisture from the humidity
in the air can turn to mold that
will rot the fabric. An air-tight
environment will encourage this
sad state of affairs.

GIMME SHELTER

Everyone needs shelter and your quilt is no different. It needs protection from moisture, heat, light, and the little creepy-crawlies that go bump in the night.

Store your quilt away from direct contact with wood. Protect your quilt by wrapping it in acid-free paper or in cloth. A cotton pillowcase or a muslin sheet is a good choice.

You wouldn't enjoy living in an attic that gets too hot or a basement that gets too damp, and neither will your quilt.

SOUTHERN OREGON HIGHLIGHTS, 65" x 59", Karen Hanken, Jacksonville, OR

Do Not Bend (Folding's OK) or Mutilate

Debates abound in the quilting world. One such debate centers around the best way to store quilts. Flat? Folded? Rolled? Crumpled? Your main concern should be to prevent permanent creases or folds from developing in your quilts.

You can lay quilts out flat on a spare bed, one on top of another.

You can roll a quilt on a tube (decorator fabric stores are a good source of these). Wrap the tube with acid-free paper first to protect the quilt from the tube itself.

FOLDING

If you fold your quilts, then refold them occasionally to prevent permanent creases from forming. Folding on the bias, or the diagonal, seems to minimize the effects of folding on your quilt.

Just like your quilts, if you were in the same position for too long, you'd get cramped, too! Refolding not only protects your quilts but also gives you a chance to touch, see, and enjoy quilts that are normally out of sight.

HEAVY METAL

That innocent little safety pin or straight pin you may be tempted to use to attach a label to your quilt is a rust stain waiting to happen. If you purchased your quilt, make sure someone didn't (gasp!) staple a price tag to it.

Remove any and all metal items from your quilt.

Lace #2, 58" x 58", Helen Stubbings, Lenah Valley, Tasmania, Australia & Tracey Browning, Ageny, South Australia

A Toe in the Water

Do some wet testing before you immerse your quilt in water. You want to see if any of the fabrics might bleed.

First, lightly brush the fabric with a dry white paper towel to see if any of the color comes off. Next, wet a Q-tip and dab it on an inconspicuous spot on the suspicious colored fabrics. If neither test shows any color, go ahead and wash your quilt.

If you are still uncertain, take the precaution of putting one of the new "dye magnets" in the water as you wash your quilt. There is also a commercial product that will keep excess dye in one fabric from settling on other fabrics during washing.

BATH TIME

To wash a quilt, you want to totally immerse it in water. This is primarily a soaking operation, not an agitating one.

Fill a sink, tub, or washing machine with cool water. If you are washing a particularly large or delicate quilt, use a bathtub, first lining it with a white bed sheet.

Add soap or a detergent especially formulated for quilts or fine linens. Immerse the quilt. If the water becomes soiled immediately, drain the water and start over. Let the quilt soak for awhile, depending on how much dirt you are trying to remove. Turn the quilt gently by hand and soak a bit longer. Drain the water, fill again, and rinse until the water runs clear.

Orange Coneflowers, 54" x 43½", Ann Fahl, Racine, WI

Time to Get Out

Take care when removing a quilt from a sink or tub. The weight of the water still in the quilt can damage delicate thread or fabric. This is why lining a bathtub with a sheet is a good idea. You can lift the sheet out, which will support the weight of the quilt.

Gently squeeze (not wring!) out as much water as possible. If it is a utilitarian quilt, it will hold up during a brief spin on the washing machine's gentle cycle.

Dry as a Bone

The safest way to dry a quilt is to lay it out flat. This allows you to block it at the same time. That is, you can smooth it into shape, making sure the edges are straight and the corners are square.

Lay a white sheet on the floor or outside on the ground. Spread out the quilt so it is completely flat and not stretched out of shape, then lay another sheet over it to protect it while it dries. If you are indoors, the quilt will dry faster if you run a fan in the same room. Turn the quilt over when it's almost completely dry so the back will dry.

Enjoy the clean, fresh smell and feel of your quilt!

ROGALAND ROSEMALING, 49" x 49", Trudy Sondrol Wasson, Eden Prairie, MN

Dry Cleaning

NO! Dry cleaning is not dry! It's a chemical bath that can wreak havoc with washable fabrics. It may well permanently set spots and stains in your quilt, to say nothing of giving it a chemical smell and un-quilt-like feel.

Non-Washable

Quilts made of non-washable fabrics, or those heavily embroidered or embellished, need to be aired and possibly shaken or vacuumed often to prevent dirt accumulation. Don't give in to the temptation to dry clean your non-washable quilts.

WOODLAND SIGHTING, 41" x 44", Cindy Vough, Nicholasville, KY

HOMELAND SECURITY

ACID-FREE PRODUCTS

Acid-free products can be your stored quilts' best friends!

Layers of tissue are recommended when folding your quilts for storage. Crunching up tissue paper and putting it in the folds of a quilt helps prevent creases and brownish staining from lack of air. However, ordinary gift-wrapping tissue paper contains chemicals that are harmful to textiles.

Acid-free tissue paper protects against acid migration and abrasion. It is available at quilt shops, museum stores, and online, as are acid-free storage boxes. The longevity of acid-free products is three years, so make a note on the tissue or box (with an acid-free pen, of course) of the purchase date so you know when to replace the old with new.

KNOCK ON WOOD

Protect your quilts from raw wood in unfinished or antique furniture. Bare wood gives off acids that can gradually damage your quilts and cause brownish stains. The same can happen with wooden dowels or the wood in an unfinished quilt frame (although surely you won't have a quilt in a frame so long as to allow that to happen!).

Sealing the wood can prevent damage caused by unfinished wood.

THE WILD GARDEN – ECHINACEA, 88" x 62", Rita Steffenson, Urbana, OH

Pipe Dream

White PVC piping is commonly used to make quilt frames that support a quilt during the quilting process. PVC contains an oil derivative that will eventually discolor your quilt. Exposure to a quilt frame is fairly short term and not usually a problem, but if you think you're not going to get back to the quilting for a while, remove your quilt from the frame.

If you want to roll a quilt around a PVC pipe for storage, first wrap the pipe in muslin or acid-free tissue to protect your quilt.

SYMBOLIC REMNANTS, 78" x 54", Carol Taylor, Pittsford, NY

LITTLE CATS IN THE GARDEN, 75" x 85", Fumie Sasaki, Tagajo, Miyagi, Japan

READ ALL ABOUT IT

It is possible to find a quilt that was made with the English paper-piecing method where paper templates were left in place. Although paper is an acid product that can discolor or degrade the fabric over time, the decision to remove the paper should be made on a case-by-case basis.

If the papers are nondescript and the fabrics are significant, try removing the papers, as long as you can do so without damaging the fabrics. Keep in mind that if the fabric is already somewhat degraded, the papers will be supporting the fabric and could be left in place. On the other hand, if the papers are newspapers or parts of letters and the fabrics are common, remove the papers and save them separately.

Paper and fabrics are not a good combination.

HERE, KITTY, KITTY

Spot may be cute,
Kitty may be sweet,
But keep them afar
To keep your quilts neat.

TEACH YOUR CHILDREN WELL

How you treat your quilts will
set an example to those around you.
Showing how you respect and handle
your quilts with care will help educate
your family and friends.

THE USUAL SUSPECTS, 45½" × 45", Nancy S. Brown, Oakland, CA

IS THAT FOR ME?

If you give a quilt
as a gift, be sure to tell
the recipient what kind
of care it requires to have
a long and happy life.
Include a special quilt
storage bag and printed
instructions on how to take
care of the quilt.

COMPLEMENTARY, 65" x 65", Gina Perkes, Payson, AZ

WHAT COULD POSSIBLY HAPPEN?

Almost anything can happen, which is why there is an insurance industry. Make sure you have a clear understanding of what kind of insurance coverage you have on your quilts, if any. Don't assume that your homeowner's policy will adequately cover your quilts. Many insurance agents view quilts as blankets and will compensate you accordingly.

Quilts of significant value can be listed separately on a special rider to your policy. Every policy is different, so ask an agent about your coverage. You'll sleep better under your quilts if you know they're adequately insured.

PLAN AHEAD

Should a disaster befall you and your possessions, it will help if you've given some advance thought on how to handle your quilt in such a situation.

Keep the quilt in your possession.

Photograph the quilt to show current condition.

Notify your insurance company.

Arrange for an assessment of damage.

Keep all receipts (appraiser charges, cleaning, restoration, or repair).

Take one step at a time as you put the loss of material things in perspective.

WHAT'S YOUR PROBLEM?

WRINKLES

Just like any textile, your quilt can become wrinkled from improper storage, washing, or use. Your first reaction might be to iron it, but *don't*! You are not dealing with a single layer of fabric. You have three layers and you may not even be sure what that middle layer is. Some battings in that middle layer could melt, adhere to the fabric, and become brittle.

Let the wrinkles hang out. A light steaming will help relax some wrinkles but be careful of using too much moisture.

SUMMER FLOWERS, 66½" x 74", Kathy Munkelwitz, Isle, MN

Dust

Quilts displayed in the open air get dusty just as furniture does. Dust mites love to nestle in textiles. Antique quilts are a haven for such little beasts.

Your sturdier quilts can be shaken out to remove the dust. The more delicate quilts should be gently vacuumed. Place clean nylon window screening over the quilt and vacuum the quilt in small sections. Vacuuming through the screening will help protect the quilt's fabrics and any embellishments.

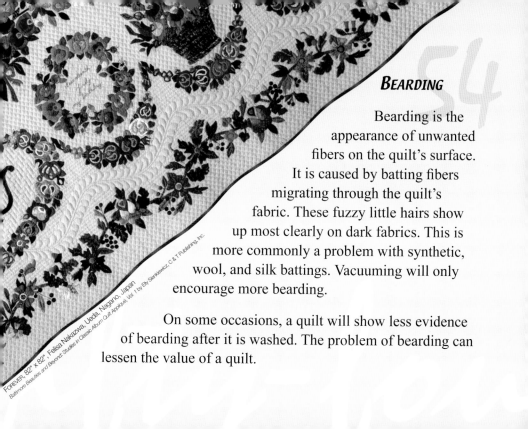

BEARDING

Bearding is the appearance of unwanted fibers on the quilt's surface. It is caused by batting fibers migrating through the quilt's fabric. These fuzzy little hairs show up most clearly on dark fabrics. This is more commonly a problem with synthetic, wool, and silk battings. Vacuuming will only encourage more bearding.

On some occasions, a quilt will show less evidence of bearding after it is washed. The problem of bearding can lessen the value of a quilt.

FOREVER, 82" x 82", Felisa Nakazwa, Ueda, Nagano, Japan
Baltimore Beauties and Beyond: Studies in Classic Album Quilt Appliqué, Vol. 1 by Elly Sienkiewicz, C & T Publishing, Inc.

SCENT OF A QUILT

A quilt is a textile and textiles pick up odors—from animals, perfumes, smoke, or that nice little bowl of potpourri sitting nearby. Antique quilts may have a musty or dusty odor.

Airing or washing a quilt can help remove any unwanted odors. Preventive measures are probably easier to set up (and enforce!) than removing odors after your quilt has picked up an unpleasant smell.

SPOTS AND STAINS

Your quilt may have acquired some age spots. (You may have, too!)

The most frequently seen spots in older quilts are from mildew, animal activity of one kind or another, insects, and acid. A lightly speckled, blemished area is most likely the result of poor storage and a lack of air. A good soaking with a soap or detergent especially formulated for quilts or fine linens may help.

SCARLET BEAUTY, 82" x 99½", Kathryn Sims, Alexis, IL
Sleeping Beauty pattern by Susan Garman, Quakertown Quilts

O POSITIVE

If you've just bled on your quilt, believe it or not, you're in luck! Why? Because your own saliva will remove your own blood from fabric.

If the stain is someone else's blood, try spot cleaning it first. If the spot is on colored fabric, you run the risk of removing the color as well as the stain. If the spot is on lighter fabric, you can be a little more vigorous in your attempts to remove it.

A WORD OF CAUTION

When dealing with spots or stains on a quilt, doing a little is sometimes better than doing too much. Start with clear water and don't let your enthusiastic efforts to remove a stain inadvertently remove a fabric's color as well.

A Little Rough Around the Edges

No matter what kind of edge treatment your quilt has—most commonly a binding or knife-edge finish—historically it will be the first part of your quilt to show signs of wear. If it is a binding that is worn, it is an easy part of the quilt to repair, either by removing and replacing the binding or by adding a new binding over the existing one.

If you are buying a used or antique quilt, the condition of the edge treatment is often the best indication of the amount of wear the quilt has had.

SMALL MEDIUM AT LARGE, 7¾" x 7¾", George Siciliano, Lebanon, PA

EARLY TO BED

A quilt you are using night after night is vulnerable to wear at the point where you pull it up under your chin. Tugging as you pull can weaken the stitching. Repeated exposure to bare skin and face creams or make-up can also be a problem.

In the past, it was not unusual to see a protective cover basted along the edges to protect the quilt from damage. Turning a bed quilt on a regular basis can minimize the accumulated damage to any one part of the quilt.

WATER DAMAGE

Water damage is easier to prevent than correct. If water is spilled on a quilt, place a white towel underneath the wet spot and pat it dry from the top with a white cotton cloth or towel. Lay the quilt out flat to air dry after you have removed as much moisture as possible.

If a quilt gets wet while being stored, the damage can include dirt or stains from dirty water (maybe a roof leak into an attic) or the storage container itself (a trunk or drawer). A good soaking while washing the entire quilt can lighten the appearance or, with luck, remove most of the stain.

A quilt damaged by a flood should be washed, not cleaned chemically.

Osgoode Hall, 68" x 68", Jean Biddick & Jo Cady-Bull, Tucson, AZ

A Stitch in Time

Just as with our clothing, the sooner something is repaired, the better. Small and timely repairs prevent a damaged area from becoming worse.

Check your quilt for weak seams, holes in the seams where the thread has broken, and loose bindings. Although these are simple to repair, you want the job done carefully. If you don't have the skills yourself, check with your local quilt shop for someone to help you or use professional services.

UFOs

In the quilt world, an unfinished project is called a UFO. This could be in the form of a few completed blocks or a finished quilt top that has yet to be quilted. If it is an antique, it may be too delicate or worn to finish and you may want to keep it as is.

Unfinished quilt tops, just like finished quilts, can be enjoyed by displaying them just as they are.

TWILIGHT DANCE, 51" x 64", Charla Gee, Littleton, CO

A THING OF BEAUTY IS A JOY FOREVER, KEATS, 77" x 77", Atsuko Griffin, Pueblo, CO
Baltimore Album Quilts: A Pattern Companion to Baltimore Beauties and Beyond; Baltimore Beauties and Beyond: The Best of Baltimore Beauties Part 1; Papercuts and Plenty, Vol. II of Baltimore Beauties and Beyond; Applaqué 12 Borders & Medallions; Patterns from Easy to Heirloom By Elly Sienkiewicz, C & T Publishing; Spoken Without a Word by Elly Sienkiewicz, The Turtle Hill Press

SUMMER QUILTS

An alternative to quilting a UFO would be to attach a backing, but no batting, to protect the back of the top from damage and support the fabrics. In the past, just such batting-less quilts were used as summer coverlets.

GETTING TO THE FINISH LINE

Consider all options for getting your unfinished quilt top quilted. Ask at your local quilt shop if hand or machine quilting best fits the style and age of your quilt top. The owner should be able to supply you with the names of reputable and skilled quilters. Ask to see samples of their work.

The shop owner will also be the best person to assist you with selection of appropriate batting, fabric for the quilt backing, and thread. You'll want to select them yourself, rather than rely on your quilter's own supply.

Meet with the quilter so she understands how you want the quilt quilted and you understand the cost and time required.

FANDANGO, 68" x 68"; Rachel Wetzler, St. Charles, IL.

USE AND DISPLAY

HANG 'EM HIGH

If you decide to display your quilt by hanging it on a wall, you want a method that will evenly support its weight. A "sleeve" is a separate length of cloth, 4"–6" wide and as long as the quilt is wide. Sew the sleeve on the back along the top edge of the quilt. Then run a rod or dowel through the sleeve, making sure it extends just beyond the sleeve.

Mount a hanging rod on the wall with support brackets or something as simple as a couple of nails.

MEETING WITH THE AUTUMN, 46" x 57", Kim Joung Soon, Taegu, South Korea

DIM THE LIGHTS!

Quilts can fade. Fluorescent lighting is a killer on fabrics, but you can purchase filters for fluorescent fixtures. Protect quilts from the heat of incandescent light bulbs by keeping your quilts 10–12 feet away from them.

Quilts on beds can fade unevenly from sunlight coming through the windows. Keep the blinds drawn to protect the quilt.

THE SUNSHINE OF MY LIFE

For temperature control and protection from light, choose an inside wall to hang your quilt.

MOVE IT!

Exposure to the same lighting, temperature, and usage may cause gradual wear or damage to a quilt that you won't even notice. But it's happening just the same. So move your quilts around. Let one that's been on a bed hang on a wall instead. Switch quilts between the rooms where they have been residing

MOUNTAIN SUNFLOWER, 47" x 47", Annie Buck, Underhill, VT

RISING SUN quilt by Carol Gilham Jones, *America's Printed Fabrics 1770-1890* by Barbara Brackman, C & T Publishing, Inc.

TRADING PLACES

Letting quilts rest occasionally is another way of protecting them. Trade a quilt that has been stored away for awhile with one that has been on display. Try changing quilts with the seasons.

Textiles react to stress, just like you do. A break in the routine or a complete vacation can be just the thing to counteract that stress.

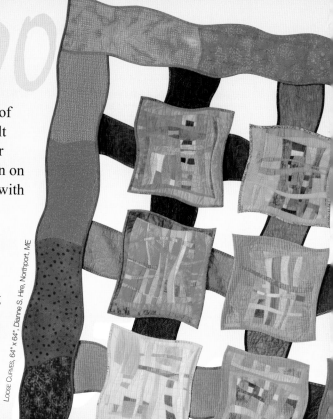

LOOSE CURVES, 64" x 64", Dianne S. Hire, Northport, ME

IT'S A FRAME UP

Framing is a wonderful option for displaying a quilt. It allows you to enjoy your quilt as art. Ask at your local quilt or needlework shop to locate a professional framer who specializes in textiles. The framer should know about using acid-free products and spacing the textile away from the glass.

Ask lots of questions about how your quilt will be handled. What will secure the quilt? Can it be easily removed? What lighting is recommended? How will non-glare glass affect the look of the quilt? Should no glass be used?

You want to be sure the framing doesn't damage your quilt. Rely on both the professional's opinion and your own taste when selecting the frame to enhance your quilt.

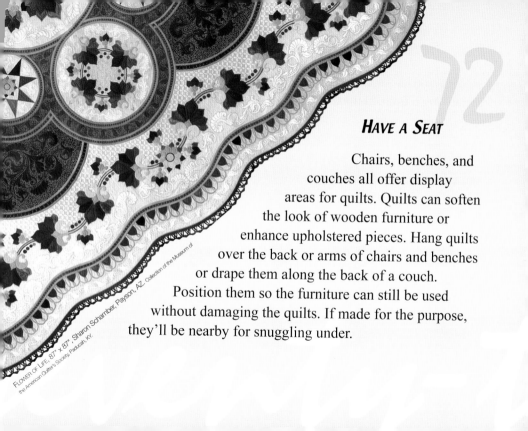

HAVE A SEAT

Chairs, benches, and couches all offer display areas for quilts. Quilts can soften the look of wooden furniture or enhance upholstered pieces. Hang quilts over the back or arms of chairs and benches or drape them along the back of a couch. Position them so the furniture can still be used without damaging the quilts. If made for the purpose, they'll be nearby for snuggling under.

FLOWER OF LIFE, 87" x 87", Sharon Schamber, Payson, AZ, Collection of the Museum of the American Quilter's Society, Paducah, KY.

RACK 'EM UP

Quilt racks for displaying quilts come in a variety of sizes and shapes. Some sit on the floor and are often designed to hold more than one quilt. A ladder leaning up against a wall can hold a folded quilt on every rung. Large floor hoops made for quilting can also be used to drape and display a quilt. There are shelves made with a rod beneath for hanging quilts.

Be sure to reposition the quilts occasionally, shaking or brushing off any dust, and refolding them to minimize the effects of being on display. Think of it as just another chance to touch and enjoy your quilts.

NOVEMBER FIELDS, 89" x 89", Gail Stepanek, New Lenox, IL.
Collection of Western Baptist Hospital, Paducah, KY

QUILTS LIVING IN GLASS HOUSES

Glass cases are available for storing quilts. Picture a chest or a coffee or end table piece of furniture with a glass top and sides, with a pile of quilts residing inside. Just be sure to refold them every now and again and they'll be perfectly happy there, adding to your décor and enjoyment.

DON'T TUCK ME IN

If you are using your quilt for a bed cover, leave all the sides hanging down straight without tucking them under the mattress or crunching the corners around the bed posts. It may have been the practice in the past, but many an old quilt shows damage from being tucked between a box spring and mattress. Rust stains and tearing are the sad result.

WHERE CAN I PUT IT?

In addition to the more obvious uses, quilts can be used as window treatments (hung with a lining to protect the back from fading), shower curtains (with a liner to protect it from moisture), table toppers (small ones), and tablecloths (larger ones).

Think outside the box when it comes to using and displaying your quilts. Remember to treat them gently and move them around or change their usage to minimize wear and tear.

THE QUILTED MANTLE, 78" x 100½", Jaynette Huff, Conway, AR

BABY QUILTS

A quilt intended for a baby should be made of washable fabrics. The fabrics should be washed before the quilt is made or given.

Antique baby quilts are fairly rare because they were made to be used and wore out before they had a chance to become an antique!

Dancin' Teapots II, 52" x 52", Virginia Anderson, Shoreline, WA

QUILTS ON THE MOVE

HAVE QUILT, WILL TRAVEL

On occasion, you may find yourself traveling by car with your quilt—to a quilt show or to visit an appraiser or even just to deliver the quilt as a gift or for sale. Your car insurance does not cover the contents of your car, should an accident happen or if someone breaks in.

Keep your quilt out of plain sight, not only to discourage trouble but also to protect it from the light. If you're traveling more than a day, keep your quilt with you at night.

An alert traveler makes for a safe trip.

NAVIGATING THE STARS, 96" x 96", Mary K. Ryan, Rutland, VT & Jan Snelling-McTaggart, Wallingford, VT
Owned by the Vermont Quilt Festival

PACK YOUR BAGS

Prepare your quilt for travel as if you were about to store it away for a short period of time. Be sure it is labeled with your name and address. Put the identification and the quilt in an opaque container before you put it in a waterproof carrier or suitcase. Keep the bag with the quilt with you as you travel.

When you arrive at your destination, let the quilt stretch out and relax, just as you would want to do after a long, cramped trip.

SHIPPING DEPARTMENT

Loosely fold your quilt and place it securely in a plastic bag to keep it from getting wet during shipping. Place the wrapped quilt in a box, tape it shut, and label it with the destination and your name and address. Then put the box in another box and seal the outer box with packing tape. Do *not* label the box as containing a quilt.

Use a reliable shipping carrier and insure the quilt for its appraised or estimated value. Ask for a tracking number and request a signature at the delivery point. Overnight shipping is the safest (and most expensive!) as your quilt will be routed differently from regular packages.

QUILTS ON LOAN

If you are lending your quilt, be sure you understand the purpose of the loan and under what circumstances your quilt will be living while it's away.

SHOW TIME

If your quilt is to appear in a quilt show, ask if the venue has insurance to cover your quilt and if there will be security at all times. It's also important to know if the quilt will be handled carefully and if it will be protected from people touching it. Be sure to specify if you don't want your quilt photographed. Have the borrower sign for the quilt and return the paperwork when the quilt comes home.

LOST AND FOUND

Many people whose quilts have been lost or stolen have been helped by the quilting community at large through the Web site www.lostquilt. com. Information about your missing quilt can be posted there. This site also has helpful information on protecting your quilts and plenty of "Happy Ending" stories about recovered quilts.

Stop, Thief!

Alas, quilts can be stolen. Report the loss of a quilt to the police and to your insurance company. Gather your documentation including photographs and any appraisals. Review in your mind who might have come in contact with the quilt or under what circumstances it might have been stolen.

TWILIGHT FRIENDS, 62" x 66", Judith Sheridan, Skaneateles Falls, NY

THE WIDE WORLD OF QUILTS

QUILT DOCUMENTATION PROJECTS

Your quilt is part of quilting history
and there are many states and organizations
interested in documenting that history.
Information about quilts reveals information
about the communities and the times in which
they were made and about the people who
made them.

Quilt shops, quilt guilds, and museums
are just a few of the organizations that sponsor
quilt documentation events. Check with your
local organizations to see if they are planning
a quilt documentation day. Your quilt and your
participation will be welcomed.

CAROUSEL CAPERS, 78" x 46½", Shirley P. Kelly, Colden , NY

Don't Be a Cut Up

Before you cut up what looks like an old or damaged quilt, consider that a quilter somewhere took time, thought, and energy to construct it. Age and wear does not automatically give one license to cut up and reconstruct a quilt.

Preserve what you can of your quilt for the next generation, instead of saving just a piece of it.

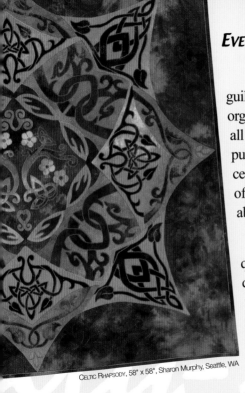

CELTIC RHAPSODY, 58" x 58", Sharon Murphy, Seattle, WA

EVERYWHERE A QUILT, QUILT

Lucky for us, quilt shows abound! Local guilds, state guilds, quilt shops, museums, and organizations dedicated to quilts and quilters all sponsor quilt shows and exhibits. Quilt publications, the Internet, highway visitor centers, quilt shops, and museums are just a few of the places where you can find information about upcoming quilt shows and exhibits.

You can find shows that feature all kinds of quilts, those that specialize in a certain kind of quilt, like art or antique quilts, and exhibits that focus on a time period or quilt artist. Shows can feature work of local artists or by quilters from afar. Quilt shows are held around the world, with more being planned all the time.

TRAINS AND BOATS AND PLANES

Is there a show you want to see that's far away? There's probably a tour that you can join that will take you there… by bus, by plane, by train, or even by riverboat!

GALVESTON BAY BLUES, 100" x 107", Island Quilter's Guild, Galveston, TX

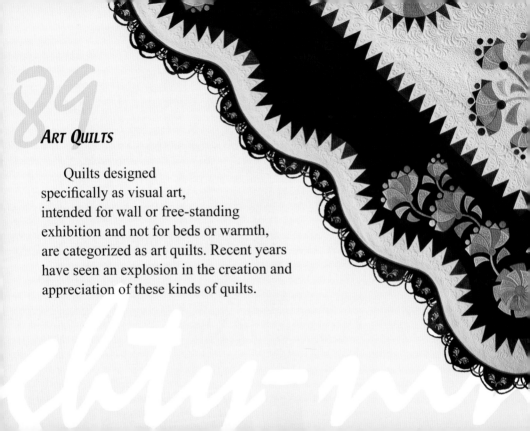

ART QUILTS

Quilts designed
specifically as visual art,
intended for wall or free-standing
exhibition and not for beds or warmth,
are categorized as art quilts. Recent years
have seen an explosion in the creation and
appreciation of these kinds of quilts.

Quilts of all kinds are
often intended to be viewed
from both sides. Quilt artists
often include piecing or appliqué
on the backs of their quilts that
complement the design on the front. They
might add embellishments such as beads,
crystals, or special threads, or do the quilting in
such a way that the back is a thread duplicate of the
design on the front.

"Ladies of the needle" have often said that the back of a
work should be as good as the front. Quilt artists have taken this
adage to heart.

SPIN DANCER, 98" x 98", Sharon Shamber, Payson, AZ

COLLECTING, BUYING, AND SELLING

COLLECTING

If you have more than one quilt, you have the start of a collection. More than likely, you will have developed a preference for a particular type, style, or age of quilt. These that you prefer are the quilts that can make up the core of your collection.

The three most important considerations in buying property are "location, location, location." With your quilts, "condition, condition, condition" is most important.

As your collection grows, "buy up" to improve the overall quality of your collection and sell off what no longer is up to the standard your better quilts set. Document each quilt in as much detail as you are able.

BUYING

If you are considering buying a quilt, try to get to know it as well as you know your own quilts. Ask the seller for as much information as they can give—where was it made, when, by whom, why, and any other details they may have.

Look for signs of wear or staining. The condition directly affects the value of a quilt. Determine in your own mind how much you are willing to pay, then see if you and the dealer can come to an agreement.

MILO'S FEATHERED FRIENDS, 80" x 80", Carol G. Benson, Barrington Hills, Il

SELLING

There are quilt dealers at shows, garage sales, flea markets, auctions, quilt shops, galleries, and on the Internet. You can look for a buyer for your quilt in any and all of these places. Selling through a consignment arrangement gives you access to a dealer's market exposure. Selling the quilt directly eliminates any third-party fee.

Determine how much you feel you need to get for your quilt. Do some research so you understand the value of your quilt in relation to current market trends. Remember that fair market is a value that is agreed to by both the buyer and seller.

EBAY

The best known and most widely used Web site for buying and selling just about anything is eBay, http://www.ebay.com. There's plenty of information out there, on the Web too, on just how to go about listing your quilt for sale. Just do a search on "selling on eBay."

ARE YOU BEING SERVED?

If you do not want to travel on the World Wide Web yourself, there are computer-savvy people who will do it for you. They know just how to photograph and list your quilt and are willing to do the research necessary to help you set a fair price.

WHATEVER DO YOU MEAN?

BATTING

The batting is the filler between the quilt top and the backing fabric that gives it the heft and dimension we associate with quilts. Today we have a wide variety of beautifully made battings to choose from in a variety of sizes and materials. In addition to cotton there are cotton/polyester blends, wool, and silk battings available.

In earlier times, just about anything was used as batting including old clothing and blankets, newspaper, straw, and, amazingly enough, corn cobs.

Fiesta De Talavera, 72" x 72", J. Michelle Watts, Roswell, NM & Rita Galaska, Alto, NM

FIT TO BE TIED

The purists may say that "it's not a quilt unless it's quilted," but there are quilts where the three layers are tied together at fairly closely spaced intervals, rather than sewn together with the quilting running stitch. The standard space between ties is 3"–4" to prevent the batting from slipping or clumping during laundering.

Tied quilts can be traced back to early quilts of thick fabrics and batting or filler, specifically made to keep people warm. They were tied because their thickness made them difficult to quilt. With a bow to the purists, tied quilts are often called *comforters* instead.

PAT REACHES QUILTERS NIRVANA, 48" x 48", Linda Cantrell, Fletcher, NC

SEDONA ROSE (back detail), 109" x 109", Sharon Shamber, Payson, AZ
Collection of the Museum of the American Quilter's Society, Paducah, KY

EMBELLISHMENTS

Any additions to the surface of the quilt top or back can be thought of as embellishments. They might include crystals, lace, buttons, embroidery, dimensional flowers, beading, silk ribbon, fringe, ruffles, yarn, or shells. The imaginative quilters of today have been known to embellish quilts with remarkably nontraditional materials including small toys, jewelry, and stuffed animals.

Nonwashable embellishments attached to a washable quilt might have to be removed before laundering the quilt. Additional care might be needed to protect the embellishments, especially if the quilt is to be folded or stored.

KEEPING WATCH

Preservation is the effort to keep a quilt safe from injury, harm, or destruction.

Conservation is the effort to stabilize a quilt that has deteriorated from its original condition and to prevent further damage from taking place.

Restoration is the effort to restore an old or damaged quilt to as close to its original condition as possible.

SEDONA ROSE, 109" x 109", Sharon Shamber, Payson, AZ
Collection of the Museum of the American Quilter's Society, Paducah, KY

WHERE THERE'S A WILL, THERE'S A WAY

What will become of your quilts after you're gone? If you have a will that specifies who gets your quilts or where they are to be donated, you will save everyone, including yourself, some headaches.

How do you choose? Think about those who expressed interest in and appreciation for your quilts. You might also consider donating your quilts to a local historical society, a favorite charity, or a museum.

You can't take them with you but you can make sure they'll be cared for when they outlast you.

THE WISHMAKERS, 53" x 60", Sue Holdaway-Heys, Ann Arbor, MI

RESOURCES

http://www.womenfolk.com/quilting_history/

BIBLIOGRAPHY

Adamson, Jeremy Elwell and Patricia S. Smith. *Calico & Chintz: Antique Quilts from the Collection of Patricia S. Smith*. Washington, D.C.: Smithsonian Institution Scholarly Press, 1998.

American Quilter's Society Appraisal Certification Committee and Bobbie A. Aug. *Protecting Your Quilts: A Guide for Quilt Owners*. Paducah, Kentucky: American Quilter's Society, 1996.

Aug, Bobbie A., Sharon Newman, and Gerald E. Roy. *Vintage Quilts: Identifying, Collecting, Dating, Preserving & Valuing*. Paducah, Kentucky: American Quilter's Society, 2002.

Aug, Bobbie A. and Gerald E. Roy. *Antique Quilts & Textiles: A Price Guide to Functional and Fashionable Cloth Comforts*. Paducah, Kentucky: Collector Books, 2004.

Brackman, Barbara. *Clues in the Calico: A Guide to Identifying and Dating Antique Quilts*. Charlottesville, Virginia: Howell Press, Inc., 1989.

Cognac, Camille Dalphond. *Quilt Restoration: A Practical Guide.* Charlottesville, Virginia: Howell Press, Inc., 1994.

Green, Mary V. *Creative Quilt Collection: From That Patchwork Place.* Woodinville, Washington: That Patchwork Place, 2006.

Gridley, Judith S., Joan Reed Kiplinger, and Jessie Gridley McClure. *Vintage Fabrics Identification & Value Guide.* Paducah, Kentucky: Collector Books, 2005.

Hargrave, Harriet. *From Fiber to Fabric: The Essential Guide to Quiltmaking Textiles.* New York, NY: Watson-Guptill Publications, 1997.

Meller, Susan and Joost Elffers. *Textile Designs: Two Hundred Years of European and American Patterns Organized by Motif, Style, Color, Layout, and Period.* New York, NY: Harry N. Abrams, Inc., 2002.

Nephew, Sara. *My Mother's Quilts: Designs from the Thirties.* Woodinville, Washington: That Patchwork Place, 1988.

Patchwork Place. *Creative Quilt Collection, Vol. 2: From That Patchwork Place.* Woodinville, Washington: That Patchwork Place, 2007.

Trestain, Eileen Jahnke. *Dating Fabrics: A Color Guide 1800–1960.* Paducah, Kentucky: American Quilter's Society, 1998.

ABOUT THE AUTHOR

Ann began her quilting career in 1970 by producing a line of patchwork products that she successfully marketed across the country. In 1979 her established business of Patches etc. turned into a quilt shop in the historic district of St. Charles, Missouri. In 1984, Patches etc. Craft Center was opened to accommodate her needlework clientele. In 1992, the Patches Button Shoppe made its debut, offering the first and only button shop in the St. Louis region.

Ann is a quilt historian, lecturer, and the author of *Pretty Polka Dots* and the *A Thought-a-Day Calendar for Today's Quilter*, as well as other articles for quilt-related publications. In addition, she has authored *100 Things to Do in St. Charles* and *100 Best Kept Secrets of Missouri*.

Her civic involvement has brought her many prestigious awards, including St. Charles Retailer of the Year and the Chamber of Commerce Lifetime Civic Award.

She is a certified quilt appraiser and serves on the board of the Museum of the American Quilter's Society in Paducah, Kentucky. Ann curated an exhibit of her own quilt collection at the museum.

Ann is married to Keith Hazelwood, a St. Charles attorney, and has two sons, Joel and Jason Watkins, and two step-sons, Robert and Rocky Hazelwood.

This is only a small selection of the books available from the American Quilter's Society. AQS books are known worldwide for timely topics, clear writing, beautiful color photos, and accurate illustrations and patterns. The following books are available from your local bookseller, quilt shop, or public library.

#7488 us$22.95

#6898 us$21.95

#6519 us$21.95

#6520 us$21.95

#6413 us$21.95

Look for these books nationally. *Call* **1-800-626-5420**

or *Visit* our Web site at: WWW.AMERICANQUILTER.COM